Inside Out

Poetic Reflections Mirrored from Life's Experiences

Kirk Hollowell

KISSED PUBLICATIONS

Kissed Publications
PO Box 9819
Hampton, VA 23670
www.kplapublishing.com

ISBN 10: 1-943833-01-X
ISBN: **13:** 978-1-943833-01-6
Library of Congress Control Number: 2016933421

DEDICATION

To my mother Virginia Boone who inspired me to be creative with sharing my life experiences through poetry as she has done.

To Tarika Green (RIP) who told me long ago to let the world hear the voice from within.

To my wife Cynthia who stands by me as the Queen she is.

CONTENTS

ACKNOWLEDGMENTS

A special thanks to Bishop Hawkins who has helped me to always keep GOD first, and to Kimberly T. Matthews-Hooker of Kissed Publications for pushing my right buttons!

PICTURE ME ROLLING

If you roll with 3DI it's do or die
You can't do it so don't even try

Did what was said couldn't be done
That's how we got to be number 1

Started at the bottom, now standing on top
With God as # 1 we can't be stopped

Some of us brothers are bound to be rich
You can't do it because we flipped the switch

Left you rights there where we started at
The lights went out and you were blind as a bat

When you opened them up we're already gone
Matt's got 3DI in another zone

It's a wrap; 3DI's #1

(now that the underdog's back on top)
(picture me…installation rvp)

SHOW TIME 2007

Now it's 2007 and the time has come.
We've stepped into the light because
We move as one.

Moving straight up, destined for the top.
You see it's God's plan and we won't be stopped.

If you come along our way you may ride too.
But working with the best, just ain't up to you.

Don't take it personal because it just
Might not be your turn.

God wrote this script,
And we all had to learn.

There's a time and place for everything,
And you just might be a tool.

Don't try to come and change things,
Just follow all the rules.

Everything is set in place;
The deed just has to be done.

3DI's on the right track,
Destined to be number one.

Many have come and some have gone,
And the ones still here may not
All carry on.

All along the way of life's dips and turns,
A few have fallen off from the hard lessons learned.

Blessed by GOD to do what we do.
Matt was first given the vision,
Now we see some too.

Now please don't get me wrong.
You must understand, the things
That we do, are not done by just man.

At the beginning of the day we first
Stop and pray, and ask that GOD will
Lead us, as we go about our way.

Now all through our day, the tests do come
And go, and if GOD is really in our life
Who do we show?

It really hasn't been easy no way, no how.
We still have to push each other to go
That extra mile.

But if you think you could be one to
Make a stand, ask GOD first to help you,
Then we might extend a hand.

Now Matt will surely tell you, that
He will hold the rope, and I'm the one
That will pull it up just in case you choke.

But if you think there's a chance, and that
Remains to be seen, that you might possibly
One day become a part of our team.

First things first and it's not just for show.
Down on your knees humbly to GOD you must go.

And if he should tell you what he's told
Each of us, then a decision has to be made

And it's really going to be tough.

To put your man down and be humble,
Humbled as you can, and lift GOD up higher
And become a better man.

Now as you sit here and I've told my 3DI story
Let it be known to one and all that only
GOD gets the glory.

A CHANCE ON LOVE

I've put my heat on the line many times before, would I do it again if love is the end?
(Love's a chance)

Hold onto love just once and life changes from what it used to be, to something you may not understand.

That alone makes the requirement to retain love just that.
(Love's a chance)

Love wants to cover you within its embrace, squeezing you into someone you may not really want to be. If intent on gaining love's attention, you must let love know it is wanted.
(Love's a chance)

Love seeks to gain its proper place among your emotions, looking for its turn in your life.
Love wants to take control and lead the dance regardless of the feelings that tell us no.
(Love's a chance)

We already know what we want to do, but loves cares not, and does what it wants to do.
Love answers to no one, is it out of control? Or is control given to only a chosen few?
(Love's a chance)

The price paid for love has been debated since the beginning of time, so this love of mine is counted priceless. Give love what it asks and it may not be given back. A small exchange for the large amount love asks of you.
(Love's a chance)

How can love be so cruel? Opening you up like a book to be read by anyone it chooses.
Love has too much power for one emotion to have. Like a violin love plays

you, and love is blind.
  (Love's a chance)

Love, in time is like the grapes on the vines; its gift is sweet until too much
is partaken.
Hold love accountable for what is left behind when all cards are laid on the
table.
  (Love's a chance)

Go all out, put it all in, you have to see where love wants to take you.
  (Love's a chance…Will you take it?)

A TIME AS THIS

I thought you knew why it had to happen this way
    I knew you thought we could make it easier
Still we know better as we walked and lived it
    We will come to be all that we are meant to be
As the smoke clears nothing was done in vain
    Matterless things like the deep cuts that once hurt
The distance traveled if only for those who choose it
    The roads walked before us by many not so unlike us
For we, as in you and me, are never to be contained
    When they change the game the end is still the same
A winner will and always will win there is no doubt
    The raised bar is in place for such a time as this
That time that never comes for the underachiever
    Step into what is written and embrace the knowledge
Know that it has always been there for you to have
    Who are we not to have what is meant to be
At one time provided to just a few as them only
    Written on the pages of life's ups and downs
Are the questions of life lessons we all need to see
    Now read the answers given through knowledge
Retain the wisdom learned from those who know
    Hold the keys to blessings for a time as this
Be all we are created to be nothing more never less
    Stand up as we lend a hand to a fellow man
Rise up my brother never to be down no more
    As we that's you and me then that's we three
Be who we are supposed to be when accounted for
    No weapon formed against us shall prosper
So it is written so shall it be done

ALL GROWN MEN

All grown men like you and me
Strong grown men we
    All grown men true to the real game
    Leading our families never to be the same
All grown men that talk the talk while walking the walk
New all grown men not money brought
    All grown men that are hard core, down for what ever
    All grown men for real, quit, give up, no never
All grown men like you've never see before
Smart gifted brothers not looking for forty acres and a mule any more
    All grown men that are reaching all our goals and dreams
    Eyes open to the fact life aint what it seems
All grown men that are sharing our gifts and talents
Giving back to the young brothers whose life swings in a balance
    All grown men who continue to live with integrity
    Now these are truly blessed grown men that we see
All grown men you haven't heard about because we've not been in the news
Sharp sophisticated brothers using all our tools
    All grown men standing on each other's shoulders pulling another up
    Covered by the blood because we've supped from the same cup
All grown men not unlike many others that walked this road before
Only this time it's different, we understand what we're here for
    All grown men not doing a new thing, just in a different way
    All grown men stand up . . . today is our day!!!

ALL OF US

When looking for those that are called to be, it may seem to be a problem if they are blind and cannot see.

Only one or two are needed, it will not to take that many. A little faith is used in places where they're known not to have any.

We should not go about our lives, still intent on the same old thing. It may make it impossible to hear, as the angles start to sing.

Amazing things can happen, when we allow GOD to win. Only because we opened the door and JESUS can now step in.

Looking at so many, that walked in front of us, trying to follow their footsteps but not knowing who to trust.

We all wanted to be someone special, so we did what we were told. We moved in a different direction hopping to save a soul.

Moving from the back, still needing a change of seasons. Walking the trails with purpose and new GOD given reasons.

Trying not to look back, staying focused and using our minds. Keep looking from the mountain top, it's just a matter of time.

Start putting the time in, asking for favor to come out. We will gain a few new things, and never turn about.

Now when old friends see us, they say how much we've changed, but all we have to say to them is, it's your choice to remain the same.

Now as the walls start coming down, we start to be at ease. As new life is set in motion we do not as we please.

It may seem to last for a moment, but it's not ever close to an end. Time is only trying to show us who we are, and that we must start again.

When the created becomes creators and can understand just who we are.
We'll expand beyond the moons and dwell near a star.

As long as we know who's leading, we should follow for he will never led astray.
The sun most surely will shine on us tomorrow, just as we walked through the rain today.

AN EAR TO HEAR

Sometimes I would tell you, but you don't want to hear

So I'll stand a little closer and whisper in your ear.

Why won't you ask yourself, so you won't have to wonder why?

What do you think the answer will be if you look them in the eye?

Never ask yourself why, if you already know what the answer could be.

You don't really know the answer that's why you're listening to me.

Today I'm speaking softly, but I know you can still hear.

Your end is not your future, when your future is crystal clear.

Seek understanding then apply it to what you know.

It will lead to greater wisdom, but to whom will you show.

The path is already set, and the trails have all been blazed.

Move into your promises, and avoid that early grave.

Hold on to those promises that prove to lead your way.

The sun is always shinning where life gives her better days.

BLACK COFFEE

I came to see her and she just walked by licking her lips.
Got love in a cup calling me to come take a sip.

        Got her attention, I must say hello,
        Best to keep it simple, it's no need that she knows.

I was just looking for daisies to push up.
She took the mission and is on the case.

        Looking for love and won't give up.
        You can see it in her eyes, it shows on her face.

Now just by touching her hands has changed my plans,
And holding her tight has meant sleepless nights.

        I surely long to have her.

This black coffee in my cup it always fills me up
And it's just enough for me to handle

        We brew well together this black coffee.

BUT I

I said I wont gonna tell no body but I can't keep it 2 my self

I kno a lot of yall wanta kno cause u asked me this b4

So Ima let u know but u wont keep it 2 ur self

C 4 u it's another matter

I was thinking that I could but I can't keep it 2 my self

And now that I've told u it's on u what you have to do

Cause I just can't keep it 2 myself I saved me and some 1 else

And it's not 4 me then to decide

'Cause I said i wont gonna tell no body but I

CRYING OUT LOUD

You've been crying out loud but no one heard you.
    Telling everyone, but no one believed you.

Trying to help them all, but no one cared.
    Close to turning your back, when no one shared.

It's been a lonely ride, but some return is due.
    How much you'll get back, is not up to you.

Keep doing what you do and make your stand.
    Understand sacrifices made, were made by mere man.

Hearts that are left wide open leads to richer days.
    Counted in the book of life, only the good ones stay.

Easy lesson learned from those who understood.
    Wrong road traveled for those who did as they would.

The spoils of the victory are for those who passed the test.
    Added and multiplied then shared among the rest.

So your crying out loud wasn't done in vain
    As the lives you changed will never be the same

DADDY'S GIRL

I know we've talked about it and I hope you can remember.
I'll try my best to keep it together through May, June, and December.

This is something very big and I really have to think,
But if I think about it too long it may make me drink.

So I've set aside those thoughts to only think of good things for you.
Just like this wedding thing that you're about to do.

For some dads it may very easy to do this father thing,
But I'm sure when my turn gets here my heart will surely sing.

So if you haven't heard me say it lately then it's long over do.
Your father really loves you and he's so very proud of you.

Daddy's little girl all grown up

DEEPER THAN THAT

The way I see it, may take a while
It's much, much deeper than that
And before I can change it, or rearrange it
To be what it's supposed to be

> Not saying it can't be done because it has
> Before, but what will it take and can I be
> Sure that it can be that and more.

Now everything I've said has been said
Before, so listen real close cause I won't
Say it no more.

> Now the last person that heard me
> Thought it was funny and he didn't wake
> Up till two days after Sunday

I haven't told everybody just a very, very few
Now lean in real close I'll tell you
What to do.

DEEPER THAN THAT 2

It's much deeper than that and how long it takes before you change that, or rearrange that to be what that is supposed to be.

Never saying that it can't be done because that has been done before, but what will it take, and can you be sure that it will be that and more.

Looking real close seeing not what you saw yesterday but being sure it will change for the better tomorrow.

Now ask yourself what will you do to insure that remains that as hard as that may be.

Seeing that it may never be as what you thought that to be. It may be more or less, but it takes time to see just that.

Now after realizing what that is, do you, can you, or i, possibly determine that it is right for us to choose that.

It was spoken like that way before someone else heard it, but never after anyone did just that.

That will always remain the question and the answer will always remain just that...because it's deeper than that!!!

EMOTIONS

Walking fast while moving slowly, not really knowing where to go. Silver tongued words never could say now parts the night where darkness lay.

If mountain top standing, fear must have no power here. The path is crystal clear. Time pushes past to be near. It waits for no man.

Not understanding life's lessons, means things become repeated. Behind closed eyes and turned heads, see what was hidden in broad day light.

Still not knowing of where life starts, is cause for missing part of the master's plan. Listen close to understand.

You must hear to see that you were chosen, and created in days wise spent. You are to become as you were meant.

As we tilt our light it is directed into his stars. We only estimate who we truly are.

A life learned lesson, processed through its time, must always lead to an outer mind expression that's real true confession.

FANTASY REAL

Looking through closed eyes trying to make things last
Want to go easy on her but she's moving too fast

    Heard the bed frame crack because the heat was on
    Fighting the smell of her perfume invading my zone

Didn't want to lose her so I tightened my grip
Felt the ache in my side when she bit my lip

    Now it's like a fantasy I thought I once knew
    Just can't help myself when she do what she do

Can still hear her laughter close to my face
Feeling her heart beat as we picked up the pace

    Sweating under the covers letting feelings ease out
    Wanting to understand what it's really about

Didn't mean to do it but the deed is done
Pulled back the covers and I'm the lonely one

    She was right in front of me and now she's gone
    Left me just sitting here holding my own

Now when I think about the things we did
I know it's a must that it all stays hide

    Just too much information for the weak to know
    They could never understand it's a repeat show

GIVE IT TO ME

If I told what I wanted would you give it to me?

If you got what you needed would you want more?

If I told you what it was would you keep it?

If you went that far could you go all the way?

If I got enough does that mean that you are satisfied?

If it felt that good would that leave room for empowerment?

If no one ever knew could you possibly tell them?

If it was lost today would you search for it tomorrow?

If you found it again could you ever let it go?

GOD KNOWS

GOD KNOWS
When you think you do but you don't
He knows you are better

GOD KNOWS
When what you meant to do
Didn't work out like you want it to
He has done it many times before

GOD KNOWS
When you want to but don't
He allowed you to have that choice

GOD KNOWS
When the gift he gave has not been used lately
He holds the light for you to see

GOD KNOWS
Why he let you think you knew when you didn't have a clue
He knew he could still love you anyway

GOD KNOWS
What it would take for you to love him back
He gave his only son

HE THAT IS

Born king of kings of everything
JESUS

For all things good he did live
JESUS

Then his life he did give
JESUS

God's man we must find
JESUS

And keep him saved on our mind
JESUS

When we are lost we all must cry
JESUS

When lifting our face up to the sky
JESUS

For he's the rock on which we stand
JESUS

To always touch the reaching hand
JESUS

HE WHO

Here he comes again but this time we're ready
He can't trip us up 'cause the plan is steady

See him coming with what he thinks is wit
Talking loud, but aint saying spit

Thinking what he thinks is big thoughts in his head
Opened his mouth and big words fell dead

If you say it once he'd say it again
Just to be sure he got his 2 cents in

What was said to him was already lost
He wants to win, but will he pay the cost

Now don't get us wrong, we like to win too
He can't win all the time, we thought he knew

Now he sees his pictures, through the lessons he thought he knew
Really knew nothing, didn't have a clue

Life holds a mirror up to his face, things not coming easy,
So he just wastes space

These lessons learned, he should already know
Just take your place and take it slow

Stop rocking the boat, he should just sit still
Then stop being fake, it's time to be real

He aint fooling anyone not even himself
Cut out the bull, before there's no one left

Sitting here thinking them same old lies

Do a new thing, he needs to compromise

We'll give a little more when he gives a lot
Put it all together and see what he's got

Getting himself together he may have time
He's got to be in it to win it; it's not just a state of mind

As he goes through this process he's just got to see
This is much, much bigger than just little he

I DID

I'm a winner because I stand on the truth
And because I've survived this game I'm living proof
You don't know me I'm known to be ruthless
Mess around with me and wind up tooth less

Seen by some but known by even less
One or two almost died trying to pass the test
If i happen to let you know, it's known by one more
But believe it's only to prepare for what may be in store

Don't try to fight it; the force is way too strong
And now it's only you standing and the rest is long gone
Left you by the wayside and went about their day
Standing with your mouth open, you better drop and pray

Down on your knees now speaking in tongue
Waiting to hear the bell ring, when it already rung
Got your head hung down cause you aint winning
But you can't go back now; this is your new beginning

Now you're thinking fast, 'cause if you're slow you lose
So think real good about the choice you choose
This race is not given to the swift nor the strong
You better choose right, you don't want to be wrong

The world keeps turning but you know not what tomorrow brings
So when it's all over and you can't hear the morning birds sing
You want them all to know you did the right thing

I LIVED MY LIFE

A child was born to live a life of plenty.
Not knowing how, I was taught by many.
As a kid I learned the city life.
I Lived My Life

Hockey, baseball, football stickball and other games,
We learned what city life had to offer.
I Lived My Life

Lived to see teenaged years that brought my
Mother many days filled with tears.
Basketball and Karate were the things they knew.
I never told them about the other things we'd do.
I Lived My Life

Learned about many religions and what other Gods people knew.
Then settled for the one true God that you know too.
I Lived My Life

Educated in a new town
I had to learn my way around.
You weren't there and it was me against the world.
I won because I graduated but it was never easy.
I grew into a man from hard lessons learned.
I Lived My Life

In manhood I first stood alone, and fishing
Helped me to understand solitude. Yes I was alone
Until flowers from heaven became you,
And we became one, and then we had two
And it was just us 4.
I Lived My Life

INSIDE OUT

Life spins a song and it was singing but
I liked to watch T.V. and just be happy.
Still life moved along with or without me.
Like old friends that turned into new ones
Who were there even when I never knew I needed them.
I Lived My Life

In or out of my control life moves on
I know because I saw my seed give life
To new seed that will grow.
I held her close I will always know
Who love is.

I Lived My Life

Now Live Yours

IS NOT ME

He looks like me, talks like me, walks like me
But me he will never be. Because you see He is not me
He acts like me, Is smooth like me, and one day will have more than me
But rich as me He may never be, because you see He is not me
Now when He sees He is not me, Life's simple things will no longer matter
And He is not me, but just like me only ten times better.

I must be all I can be just to prove to Him that it can be done.
Then He will see that He Just like me can be the example for his son
He is not me, and says that he no longer wants to be like me,
As his pockets keeps getting fatter. How can this be?
Did he not really see the way was paved for him, or for him it never
mattered?

Down off my high horse I did fall, but to truly fail has not been my call
He not me is not what I see, when I stand to answer for it all, but he not as
tall
He did not stand at all, for he is not me, but is all that we see though he
could not fall
I now ask you all, Could He be me? Did my eyes fail to see what I knew
was from me?

Thinking now that He is me and I am He, Is this like it's supposed to be?
No longer wondering when I still see Him trying to be like me only
different, who am I to disagree?

He's got to be He
And I've got to be me . . . For sure He is not Me

IT AIN'T OVER

Reaching for a snow flake trying to hold past times
    Watching real close as the beauty unwinds
        Pearl black rivers shinning crystal clear
            Understanding that GOD the Creator is working here

Frozen dreams looking for fresh rivers to flow
    Evolution of one's life we're all trying to know
    Content moments in the mind changes places one for another
        As part of the universes puzzle gives life pushed from the mother

Searching each second of time where the world stands still
    Asks the stature of men to act not as they want but as they are willed
        Covered under the darkness that cannot compete with the light
            Understanding removes the questions of what is wrong and
            not right

Answering any questions that is opposed to conquering your fear
Knowing life's journey is never over even as the end pushes to be near

IT IS WHAT IT IS!

If what you don't know won't hurt you
Then what will knowing do?

    If you get what you pay for
    Then who steals?

If nothing lasts forever
Then how long does something last?

    If you think you will, you will
    Then if you think you don't why don't you?

If winning is not everything
Then why play the game?

    If what you see is what you get
    Then why is love blind?

If what goes up must come down
Then why not wait?

    If you reap what you sow
    Then why not plant the best?

If forever is for always
Then how soon will ever come?

    If the sun shines on everyone sometimes
    Then does mean words really hurt you?

If what goes around comes around
Then why go backwards?

If all is fair in love and war
Then why won't women teach men how to play the game?

If there is a reason for everything
Then where is the way to everything?

If actions speaks louder than words
Then who reacts to quiet people?

If you knew then what you know now
Then why make the same mistakes more than once?

If it's going to hurt you more than it does me
Then why can't we end this with I'm sorry?

If a bird in the hand is worth two in the bush
Then how much is a cat in the hat worth?

If you shouldn't count your chickens before they're hatched
Then how could you count on someone laying an egg?

If your eyes are bigger than your belly
Then how big is your mouth?

IT'S ME

I left here and went right into now
    Do you feel me?
I'm saying go ahead, touch reality as you step into life.
    Can you see what I'm saying?
The air is free, where a breath is priceless.
    You heard me?
Oh Yea I'm deep
    Dig me if you can
I'm inside out and off and on at the same time
    Questions? I didn't think so
The answers are right here in front of you
    Get with me if you dig my flow
I'm all over; I'm here, there, and everywhere
    I'm hot baby and you're not

Talk to me now or hear me later

IT'S TIME

Time to do what you've got to do,
A few were made for this and will push through.

It's not a hard thing going through long labor.
It's a money thing with all cards placed on the table.

A price needs to be paid,
Will you be the one to do it, or just continue to work like a slave.

You were made for this and it's time to get it done.
Don't be afraid because you start as just one.

If you walk up the road the chosen will follow.
We must pass through all doors with keys to tomorrow.

Who so ever will does exactly what they say.
You can't live for tomorrow by just making it today.

This plan was set in place such a long time ago,
And that's why you couldn't see all you had to know.

Now when you look toward your future you'll see it's much brighter than
your past.
As each day gets better you'll stop looking at the last.

Listening from within, it's from a higher calling.
No time to rest right now a slip could led to falling.

Goals have to be set and at last finally reached.
Lives need to be changed, by living what you preached.

There's a time for everything and everything in due time.
Nothing remains the same when you don't press rewind.

If there was something you could say today to remove past pain, hurt and sorrow,
You would have said it years ago, now step through to tomorrow.

The Future Is Bright, Shine On!

JETTING

Jetting on the fast track going really fast
Slam on the gas trying to make a fancy pass

Shot around the first curve nice and easy
Passing two cars they calling me breezy

Took a little glance in the rear view mirror
Down shift to second cause they're getting nearer

Bumped one sucker and knocked him off track
Gotta win this race can't cut no slack

Headed for the back stretch, pushing it to the floor
Dipped to the inside, passed four more

Looking down the straight away I see the finish line
That's when that number one hit me from behind

Just for a second I'm thinking I was through
But I'm better than that, so I know what to do

I leaned to the right and made some sharp turns
Looking out the window I see cars flip and burn

I'm heading for the finish line 'cause it's all about me
Standing in the winner's circle, I count the money

KINGDOM

What you see is not always what you get

What you get may not be what you want

What you want is more than what you need

What you need is all that you deserve to have

What you deserve to have is enough for you to handle

What you can handle is more than enough for someone else

What someone else has is not really what GOD has for you

What GOD has for you is found in learning through the kingdom
KINGDOM

KNOW WHAT YOU CAN DO

Now don't make me tell you
Later that I told you so

And if you get put out front
You know you got to go

Just drop and kiss my . . .
When you pass by

Now if that's not enough for you oh, well
Don't make me puff your lip up or make your eye swell

I got things on my mind, got no time for you
So if you don't know by now

You know what you can do

LET THE TELLERS TELL AND THE SAYERS SAY WHILE THE DOERS DO

(TELL IT)
LOOKING 4 FOREVER

Thinking of a master plan,
Like picking out crystals from grains of sand
    No two are alike, yet they all seem just right.
    Not throwing up my hands to fight, but picking up this pen to write.
No two thoughts are the same,
As the wind blows and the water flows it's all subject to change.

Who really knows, the path we all chose are roads that lead to forever.

LOVE LOVED ME

I never knew she loved me.
If I did I would have never did what I did.
I thought love would let me see her before she covered me with her embrace.
I was looking for love in all the wrong places, but she was hidden in pain's view.

Love courted me but I only wanted to jump her bones, over and over again.
She never complained about how I left her wanting more, and if she did I refused to hear because I was blinded by her beauty.
I wanted to see her naked when she came to me always fully dressed to kill.

Love needed to understand clearly what I was getting into, and I needed to get straight to the point.
She loved deeply, requiring far more than I thought I had in me all those times.

Love had only scratched the surface of my soul and it drove me to question all things I thought I knew.
She opened me up for the world to see just how venerable I could be.

As all men will surely learn that love don't love nobody.
We must still give her our best at all times.
We can taste her sweet nectar or be left outside looking in.

Love opens herself up to us like the flower's pedals receive sunshine after the rain.
She is needed for our growth to be completed, and we are again whole.
I never knew why love loved me, but now I know that she really cared!

MAMA

Mama is our queen you see
She ruled on her throne with grace and dignity
She taught us to do the things a woman should
It brought us a great life like she said it would

When Mama would speak we'd linger on her every word.
Those words settled in us as we grew,
Oh Mama how we wanted to be a grown woman just like you.

Even when Mama would scold us a many of times
Her love always stayed steady, only touching those daring lines.
We only have to remember that kind of love you gave,
For it taught us early as women, how we are to behave.

We learned to see love in our faults with one another.
And although we never wanted to, you made us love our brother.
Mama you were always demanding that we finish what we start.
Your love was given with understanding, planted deep within our hearts.

Yet and still your love was real and we'll never let it steal away
Here is where your love will always stay.
Now we are grown and Mama is gone, we are prepared for what
Life will have in store, we love you Mama even more.

Mama, you will live on into tomorrow, as we too will pass through
This pain, sadness, and sorrow, because we just like you will always
Carry that true love inside. That's the real love that life won't let us hide
We love you for being our MOTHER

ME AND MY BROTHER

Me and my brother was cool like that,
We both had cowboy guns and matching hats.
We did things no one else could do.
Our bound was thick, you couldn't break through.

He wanted to be like me and I wanted to be like him
Put us together and we are better than all of them.
I taught him just like he taught me, we taught each other
On what type of man we wanted to be.

We were the best at whatever we tried to do,
Go get your brother and we'll whip y'all too.
We got whippings because of each other,
Rarely from Dad, but you can count on it from our mother.

We fought neighbors, friends, cousins, and of course other brothers.
Come one or come all, we protected one another.
Win lose or draw we stood together,
We are undefeated in our front yard in all types of weather.

Through the thick and the thin, he's been my best friend.
He's my little brother, and I'll love him till the end.
LOVE YA MAN !!

ME OR YOU

I do what I do cause I can
    I stand tall when I walk 'cause I'm a man
        You drop down when I pass 'cause you're a fan

You say what you gonna do but you don't.
    You want what I have but you won't

It's not a game that I play so I win
    You try holding my hand but no friend

It's not easy being me but you don't see
    With us all together who stops we

When I stand at the top I look down
    When you tell what you got who's around

I know you heard what I said 'cause I talk loud
    You are not in my lane 'cause you follow that crowd

I said what I said so I'm through
    Now who's right and who's wrong me or you
        (Message from the mind / tick tock goes time)

MY COUNTRY NOT YOURS

My country tears from me
Sweet land of bigotry
Of thee I sing
Land where my fathers died
Land where my brothers tried
Let freedom see
See at last see at last
Thank God almighty
We see at last

NASTY GIRL

I never had a feeling she was up to no good,
But I just had to have her, like she knew I could.
Did it all in one night, and we sure knew it was good.
She did me like nasty girls do, but not like she said she would.

We were both knocked down shaking and struggling for breath.
I knew what I was doing, but I wasn't doing it by myself.
We gave it all till there was nothing left.
I only wanted her for me, couldn't deal with anyone else.

She came with everything she had and I
Left with more than what I needed.
With every day that goes by, new tears I never cry,
But I feel the pressure from inside.
Ride nasty girl ride, she never said goodbye, no tears in these eyes

She did what she did, because I do what I do,
 No tears to cry,
 No questions to ask why.
Now feelings that lasted for a minute are in it,
 So we smile as we may pass by,
 And we try, but we live a lie.
It's now a big problem I can't deny.

Nasty girl loves all the time, unaware of love for real
Here, mad love takes too long to heal
And it leaves wounds open in the heart forever dear.
 So there's no need to ask her why
 She keeps on passing me by, yet
I sit quietly waiting for her reply.

As a nasty girl, she's one of a kind.
I came to make her mine, but I couldn't wait forever.

Chased a feeling given in a moment of pleasure,
    She was down for whatever.
We did it until it was done, so we did as much as we could.
You got to know it was all good.

Never had a reason to feel any doubt,
Nnever felt a need to do without.
So now I'm missing her like the flowers miss the rain.

Still she's nothing I can't live without,
Just more things to figure out,
Really don't need all this endless pain.
I just need to be with her again . . .

Have you seen her?

NEW BEGINNINGS

I opened my eyes but still I did not see all the good things GOD has done for me.

I stood up and took what I thought was a big step, oh but I never moved an inch without GOD's help.

GOD is good as we all well know. He gave me new life and watches me grow.

I know I'm not at the point GOD wants me to be. So I'm standing up straight for the righteous to see.

No… I'm not perfect, or without fault. I'm learning GOD's plan. I need to be taught.

My God is a forgiving GOD who always lets me know, that he is the answer, and to him I must go.

GOD is the answer for all that I may need. For in me he has planted faith, the size of a mustard seed.

So when you see me and I still appear the same, listen real close as I call out his name.

JESUS, teach me, fill me, make me whole, forgive me lord, please save my soul.

When it's all been said and done, when my life's story has all been told, may I walk with my LORD and Savior through the pearly gates and on the streets of gold.

NEW BLACK MEN

Black men like you and me
Strong black men we
>Black men true to the real game
>Leading our families never to be the same
>>Black men that talk the talk while walking the walk
>>New black men not money brought
>Black men that are hard core, down for what ever
>Black men for real, quit, give up, no never
Black men like you've never seen before
Smart gifted brothers not looking for forty acres and a mule any more
>Black men that are reaching all our goals and dreams
>Eyes open to the fact life aint what it seems
>>Black men that are sharing our gifts and talents
>>Giving back to the young brothers whose life swings in a
>>balance

Black men who continue to live with integrity
Now these are truly blessed black men that we see
>Black men you haven't heard about because we've not been in the
>news
>Sharp sophisticated brothers using all our tools
>>Black men standing on each other's shoulders pulling
>>another up
>>Covered by the blood because we've supped from the same
>>cup
>Black men not unlike many others that walked this road before
>Only this time it's different, we understand what we're here for

Black men not doing a new thing, just in a different way
Black man stand up…today is our day

NEW LIFE

Now dealing with what you have, while longing for much more

With eyes closed tightly afraid to walk through life's door

Not knowing what could happen or willing to take that chance

Still seeking to be happy and learn life's new dance

Watching it happen for others just waiting for your turn

Could it happen like that for you or is there more to life to learn

So as you read these words thinking life has given your gifts to another

You must move to take those new steps for you to go much further

New life… My life or yours

NEW MAN

Real man, man that I am
Made man, GOD's man that I am, stand man, stand because you can.

Be all man as you reach out and give a hand real man that I am.

Speak man; speak as only you can the words that lead to your destiny.
Real man that I am, I see now with eyes no longer blinded by unknown
facts, but through new vision.

Clear skies rush in and changes my thoughts of past relations, hear man,
man that I am.

Leave away with distant memories that still want to remain near.
Hear now with an ear to hear.

I stand new man!

NOT A GOOD DAY

Here he sat with a swollen eye.   Threw a hook
And started to cry.

Did not see the left jab coming, only hoped the
Hook had stunned him.

Bob and weave, he heard them say…oops a bit
Too late to do today.

For the right cross was in his face, and his
Front teeth did make a space

To grab and hold was the best thing to do,
But he's off balance, can't stop the 1-2

Didn't really see that straight 3 coming.
Might have been safe if his feet start running.

Tried with his will and tried with his might,
But knew deep inside it was a bad, bad night.

So he closed his eyes to make it go away, that's
When he woke and found it was today.

So to him just like to you I say…stick and move
Champ…stick and move; today's not a good day!!

NOW LAY ME DOWN TO SLEEP

Now lay me down to sleep
I pray the lord my soul to keep
If I should die before I wake
I pray the lord my soul to take

Now lay me down to sleep
Lord let me wake with new life on my mind
Not ever to think it could be my time
To GOD I'm faithful so I do my best
Life's in his hands my mind's at rest

I pray the lord my soul to keep
Now on my knees I do pray
Thanking the lord for a new day
Never knowing how long it will last
What's done is done it's in the past

If I should die before I wake
Before I close my eyes I pray
Thank you lord for this given day
If I didn't do all things just right
I pray for forgiveness as I lay tonight

I pray the lord my soul to take
Now as I'm drifting off to sleep
Thinking of new goals tomorrow I'll reach
It's not as if I didn't know GOD's true mercy he's bound to show
For in his words he has spoken
And gave new life if you are chosen

ON PURPOSE

In the beginning there was nothing but GOD so there was everything. So with GOD being in you, you are everything GOD has made you to be, just not yet.

I, you, me, he, she, we, all of us mean something to GOD therefore we all have a purpose, still we may not know. We move on, on purpose.

Not understanding, not meaning not to know, but still seeking purpose. Searching for tomorrow, only to find that today may be already gone.

Seeking to find what is not lost, but within your grasp just beyond finger tips. It must lead to a better understanding of self, who is to know but you? These are things done on purpose.

Soon blended thoughts will seem to flutter lightly as leaves will be lifted by winter's winds. The changing of leaves turn to changing into long sleeves, it's much more than just weather, but things done on purpose.

Not knowing when it could end, it is better to go all out. You must understand it was all part of GOD's plan because GOD does everything ON PURPOSE !

PAINTED PICTURES ON THE WINDOW SILL

Life holds a candle so softly within her hands.
It opens the eyes of every man to GOD's given plan.
Painted pictures on the window sill.

Crystal clear waters push white driven snow.
Like the spirit of new life it must be free to flow.
Painted pictures on the window sill.

No longer sleeping in deep waters where breath is labored.
Now awake with open eyes that see above the clouds.
Painted pictures on the window sill.

Remembering not what passed when leaning into the future.
Allow light to shine into darkness to see new paths through life.
Painted pictures on the window sill.

When travelling far yet not knowing where to go.
One must follow to lead or be left wondering why only you know.
Painted pictures on the window sill.

It is best that we all know.
I painted pictures on the window sill a long time ago.

PASS IT ON

Keep talking to those people about these things that was said.
Make it a short story before someone gets mad.

They're sure to let you know when enough is enough.
Just take a seat and watch them strut their stuff.

Looking from the beginning the tone was already set.
They couldn't hear it like they haven't heard anything yet.

A lot of folks keep talking but haven't shown anything at all,
How many will be standing if one takes a fall.

Is it about these stories you keep trying to tell,
Who will pay the price when it's time to pay for bail.

All these great things they know you knew,
Was meant for someone else, given through you.

It was never just to be for their life alone,
It was always a blessing to be passed on.

PEOPLES

My People, Your People, Our People
They think they know us so very well
    My People
    Your People
    Our People
The ones that give us so much hell
    My People
May not be around when you need them
    Your People
They show up just when you see them
    Our People
Act like fools but it's just them being them
    My People
    Your People
    Our People
They seem to just run and hide
    My People
    Your People
    Our People
If you pay some will stay for the ride
    My People
Always talking about what can you do for them
    Your People
Will stay at your house when it's a hundred of them
    Our People
Won't show up because you live too far away
    My People
    Your People
    Our People
Always talking about how proud we are
    My People
    Your People
    Our People

Are all on the same team until too many drinks at the bar
    My People
    Your People
    Our People
Always ready to put on a show
All these people are not like other people and this you must always know

PRETTY RICKY

Pretty Ricky is what they called him. Big fro, light skinned, green eyes, picking up all the ladies then dropping them by the way side.

Getting around is what he really tried to hide, because pat 'em and turn 'em was his only ride. That's not a thing Pretty Ricky wanted the ladies to know. So how did he say again he was gonna take 'em to the O-Jays show?

Pretty Ricky tried to dress to impress, but his style was way off base. All Pretty Ricky had going on was as he would say; his oh so pretty face.

Pretty Ricky was known to have a weak rap game not learned from a book, but he had mastered the eye glaze and for some chicks that was all it took.

Pretty Ricky was in style for a while like the flavor of the week at the corner ice cream store. Once you became the star attraction everyone knew what you tasted like. So you were for free and no one wanted you anymore.

Pretty Ricky wanted to make poor girls dream, and rich girls' cream, so preying on Betty Boo to make her scream was his thing. Hit 'em and miss 'em put 'em in his sling.

When the truth be told, you can only talk the talk but for so long. Sooner or later you've got to walk the walk. It's a learned skill, not store bought.

Pretty Rick pressed on with no game in hand. Lifting up any skirts he could, with no thought out plan. Now any wise man knows this is not the route to take if the game is to win, but you couldn't tell Pretty Ricky spit way back then.

Not Pretty Ricky, lick 'em then stick 'em was his only battle cry. If she was willing and her girlfriends too, there's no telling what he'd try to do. Two for one or one for all five, many fell victim to his bull and jive.

Pretty Ricky was getting it on like heavy weight fights; it was scheduled for

12 rounds but subject to end early. Even threw it on the crap table of life with big Shirley with no ending in site. Now we all knew that just won't right.

Pretty Ricky had haters. That's nothing new, but when your haters give it up too, what's a man to do? Doing all he could with all that would, the word got out Pretty Ricky was just really no good!

Pretty Ricky wasn't worth a dime. Had a very short fuse and didn't take his time. All about what was in it just for him. Left you at the starting block and beat you to the end. Oh so sad when the ladies put the word out. Now what's that about?

Pretty Ricky's days of hitting and quitting had come to an end. And if there was a moral to this story: "just because you can, don't mean you should" . . . but if you do, you've got to satisfy them all!!!

REAL LIFE

Try buying time looking for glory,
Told somebody but not the whole story.

Time keeps moving fast while you moving slowly.
Looking for Jesus because he's holy; holy.

Now you're out there floating in the deep end,
Still sin by most but who's your friend.

Seen by the enemy as just a mere man,
But still walking right, trying to follow god's plan.

Keep your head up, no looking down,
Push that shield up and march to the crown.

One king's glory is not yours to take.
Listen to the words, more changes to make.

Not overnight it shall all take some time,
Keep moving forward with a focused mind.

Open up your book to god's precious story,
It is all so true; to him we give the glory.

To all those who seek it, it shall be revealed
As to those who turn away life stands still.

Life's better choices are given to those that do,
Stand in the gap as life challenges you.

RIGHT NOW

It's time to do what you've got to do.
You were made for this you must push through.
It can be a hard thing going through long labor.
All money is not good money when it comes under the table.
    A price had to be paid, and you always knew it.
    Now you must understand you are not the one to do it.
    You were made for this and it's time to get it done.
    Never be afraid because you are not the only one.
If you walk up the road the chosen will follow.
Walk through that door with your keys to tomorrow.
Who so ever will, does exactly what they say.
You can't live for tomorrow by just making it today.
    This plan was set in place such a long time ago,
    And that's why you couldn't see all you had to know.
    Now when you look toward your future, you'll see it's much brighter than your past.
    As each day gets better you'll stop looking at the last.
Listening from within, can you tell it's from a higher calling?
When stepping out in faith it may feel as if you're falling.
Now new goals have to be set and at last finally reached.
Many lives need to be changed by practicing what you preach.
    There's a time for everything and everything happens in due time.
    Nothing remains the same when you stop pressing rewind.
    Do the things today to remove passed pain hurt or sorrow.
    Prepare for your future now as you walk into your tomorrow.

The future is bright shine on right now.

SEARCHING

Looking for a way out and it comes from within
Searching for that rainbow but don't know where to begin

Lifting up that heavy load but with legs that are paper thin
Calling on some old friends but they from way back when

Got yourself on your shoulders so you better hold on tight
It's scheduled for twelve rounds like it's a heavy weight fight

Don't know who to trust because nobody looks just right
Can't stop to rest a bit not even for a night

Been searching in some old mail trying to see who I told
Keep seeing the same faces since I was nine years old

People all around me keep pressing real close
Now where do you find them when you need them the most

SEE WHAT I SEE

(It's a canon thing you can't understand)
Say man, open your eyes can't you see?
Somebody just left the gate open; it's time to be free

You can stay if you want to and be just like them,
I'm moving on; can't be stuck on no limb

Not getting paid what I'm worth, and working when I shouldn't,
Just scared to tell Boss lady I know that I couldn't

You know you just promised to take your kids to the show,
But you're working overtime and now you can't go.

Got to make that money, 'cause bills got to be paid,
But what about the promise to the wife and kids, you just made

Things will get better just keep working you'll see.
Yea that's what they said then to you and to me.

Did they tell you my brother about the other plan?
Oh yea the other plan… what you didn't know?
You're being replaced and soon you've got to go.

But you've done what they wanted, why can't you stay?
You'll even work longer hours for much less pay.

Yes that's right; the other plan is coming into view.
They're replacing you and your buddy, I thought you knew.

Being replaced by the cheaper man. He works harder and don't complain
like you do.
They brought him in last week, you trained him didn't you?

INSIDE OUT

So you can't stay you've surely got to go,
So be a good boy, don't put on no show.

Guess all that butt kissing you did just didn't mean a thing,
Cause you were too busy to hear the fat lady about to sing.

Yea I know you thought it was for me,
With your eyes wide open you still couldn't see.

It's a powerful thing this downsizing can do.
They went on by me and came and got you.

I guess I'll see you when I see you; the fat lady is starting to sing.
Don't look so sad, a grown man crying is a sad, sad thing.

SHE USED TO BE MY GIRL

She was my girl and I was her guy, and we made sure everyone knew it. If you saw me you saw her, and if you saw her you would soon see me. Together forever, but that was when, she use to be my girl.

There was no me without you, and no you without me. That's the way we wanted it to be, but that was when she use to be my girl.

Love had no ending and we were only beginning, so we let love just rock our world, but that was when she use to be my girl.

When she cried I cried, when I cried we both cried. We cried together and vowed to make it better, but that was when she use to be my girl.

She let me be the man I was trying to be, and I let her be the woman she became to be, but that was when she use to be my girl.

I gave her all I had to give because she gave me more than she could and it must have drained us because love left us weak, but that was when she use to be my girl.

We were holding on tight when the world came against us, and us was all we had, we stood alone. We didn't know we couldn't make it. But that was when she use to be my girl.

Out of the blue love decided it was time to leave and go away, and me without you and you without me became our new song. I never knew what went wrong, but that all happened when she use to be my girl.

SOME MORE WORDS

Standing by the fact that you don't know thee
    It's obvious; you only see what you see
        Standing two inches from you breathing what you breathe
            But you're sucking for air 'cause he got what you need

Jumped to the front
    Just to get pushed back
        Kinda hard to face the facts
            When he knows you're better than that

Talking about something you thought you heard
    Better listen real close to God's spoken word
        Now everything ain't for everybody this you should already know
            So stop talkin' about it cause only time will show

Stand on up and get back in line
It's a done deal cause God's got you this time

SOMETHING OR NOTHING

Have you ever tried to do something and failed
And even though you look ok, you never tell

There may be trouble on every side, but
Who would know because from yourself you hide

Every now and them, things go alright
But when your spirits are low, you cry at night

The bright sunshine starts a new day
A good way to end it is to knell and pray

Changes for everyone just come and go
Like that last day of summer before a winter snow

Some days start as smiling faces
But people in it, just go through passes

It's nothing new you've seen it before
Like life's candy from the corner store

Starting at the beginning and going back again
What you thought was the start is really the end

Keeping in prospective what you wish for another
If you fail yourself have you failed your brother

It's not how you start; it's how you end
If you start at the beginning, stay till the end

SOMETHINGS

Loved somethings
Arranged somethings
And told many about it

Did somethings
Changed somethings
And left no doubt about it

Been in somethings
Went with somethings
And learned to do without it

Had somethings
Lost somethings
And felt the same about it

Asked somethings
Was told somethings
And found out less about it

SUGAR BABY, SWEET GIRL OF MY DREAMS

Sweet caramel cream
With slick hair that streams

> Dark and lovely bitter sweet
> With candy coated high arched feet

Butter ball round
Deep chocolate brown

> Cherry centered treat
> Too good just to eat

Whipped cream covered
Secret center discovered

> Mounds that go down
> Down to her feet

She melts in your mouth not in your hands
Too good to be with just any man

> Rock candy hard body not seen by just anybody
> Too cute for your boys to know

Star light eyes that show no surprise
As liquid lips with kisses she does blow

> On tiny slim waist my hands I do place
> She's compelled to give a small taste

A cute little nose that I do suppose
Sits comfortably on her face

INSIDE OUT

Butterscotch skin tells me where to begin
As a well-placed touch could mean so much

A kiss of love I may dare taste
Sour apple expressions shows on her face

As we sway through timeless passionate oceans
Mint julip hips quiver from well-placed finger tips

That I know best where to place
Trying hard to hide feelings from inside

That outward she does show
Yes always yes she never says no

Lemon tear dropped eyes truly hypnotize
But it's the quiver of legs that really know

Chocolate kisses on her face I did rain
Held her far too long not easing the pain

Until sun rising lights say good bye to the night
Her embrace I not easily let go

I look for lipstick stains on my pillow

THE 2009 GRIND

(Destined for greatness)

It's 2009 and a different grind. Looking for more good men, but they're hard to find

A few come along and they think they know. They stick around a few weeks and then out they go.

It's hard to understand when the faces keep changing, but GOD's doing his thing it's called rearranging.

So it don't matter who comes and who goes. Just looking for the brother who thinks he knows.

3DI baby we stay on the grind. Destine for big money, it's just a matter of time.

Long time put in for the times without. We stay on the grind, GOD's working it out.

GOD is opening doors looking for time well spent. I keep telling these brothers 3DI is heaven sent.

Now back to the grind, because this all must know, if you work for 3DI it's not just for show and when you hit them steps with that file on your back you gonna think to yourself this aint worth all of that.

But you saw the matching colors and the slick new shoes, and thought to yourself you could do what we do.

So you came looking for favor not knowing favor aint fair. Trying to do just a little work and wear what we wear.

You've got to understand these color come with a cost, blood, sweat, and tears and a real ugly boss.

Stay hard on the grind and stand tall in line. Stay steady; the course we will win in time!

If you've ever said "anything is possible" you've got to know what that meant......look its 2009 and we've got a black president!!!

I've said it many times before and I'm saying it again I'm grinding with 3DI and I'm all in.

Destined for greatness

Ya heard !!!!!!!

THE BROTHERS

Brothers, brothers trying 2 get ahead
Brothers, brothers they trying to count you as being dead

Looking 4 some brothers that's looking 4 me
Asking about some brothers that will step up 2 be free

Step up to the plate and take your stand
Knowing what to do to become the better man

Brothers, brothers down 4 whatever
Brothers, brothers will they quit…no never

They say they saw you falling off the path, going where you shouldn't go.
Tell me brothers was that just 4 show

Saying you'll never amount to nothing, good for not 1 thing.
Telling you if you listen, the fat lady's about 2 sing.

Brothers, brothers they want you at the back of the line
Brothers, brothers tell them no, it's not happening this time.

THE GLORY

Some things happen for a reason
Yet we can't understand
Though some move on with their lives
Many still need a hand

Life's not always easy and not
All life's lessons are learned
Some people go on through life
And the bridges they crossed are burned

Still not many could do what I did
And still not understand
Yet others still thought they knew
But again I am only man

You are who you thought you were
Only seen different from the rest
And though I may take a while
I will pass life's test

You on the other hand
Well that might be another story
Yet in a blink of one's eye lives are changed
When GOD's given the glory

THE SITUATION

The situation is what it is
Understanding that knowing is only half the part
You must know which way to go way before you start

The situation is what it is
Check the road signs; it's filled with sharp turns
Hard lessons learned if you crash and burn

The situation is what it is
Dead end signs don't always mean stop
Moved to go a different way if the journey is to the top

The situation is what it is
Setting the plans and following them through
Knowing the haters are just waiting on you

The situation is what it is
Thinking just that could bring you to tears
Left standing frozen chilled by your fears

The situation is what it is
Distant road signs seem cloudy not clear
Searching for brighter days as a change is near

The situation is what it is
Do what you must as you say what you may
Understanding just who has given this day

The situation is what it is
A day to do all that has to be done
We stand as Man in victories that we all have won

THE START OF A NEW BEGINNING

The start of a new beginning is going beyond the boundaries of what you think is as far as you can go.

That push up the ladder, that step across the gap filled with uncertainty.

That surge to the top, making the moves to make you free from the void of not knowing.

Nothing can stop you if you try. If the will is there you must try.

Never stopping to ask why, just knowing in the end it will all be better.

Launched off into the deep, Pushed beyond the limits of how far you thought you could go.

Standing by the fact that you're not alone, led by the truth of understanding.

Now thinking before reacting.

Deep thoughts rushing to the surface, plunging you over some will that held you back

The ordinary is not indifference when fiction becomes fact.

Seeking the start of a new beginning is only as far away as you yourself allow it to be.

God himself has created in you the will to overcome what you felt as limits but only if you so desire.

Understand why, not how what was once thought lost has already been found yet you hid it from yourself.

While seeking understanding, an added measure of grace along with the abundance of mercy has sustained you.

Now GOD, as in the beginning, has chosen you to stand perched at the tip of his mighty finger. You will manifest into what he has made you to be

You are now at the start of a new beginning.

THE TRUTH SHALL MAKE YOU FREE

The truth stands alone, although it may not always be told
The truth stands alone, and it already has saved your soul
    The truth is a planted seed that covers all needs
    The truth is also known to uncover dirty deeds
The truth when told won't need any support
The truth when not told will see you in court
    The truth is what it is no more, no less
    The truth is what it is will you pass the test
The truth shall make you free, free indeed
The truth must be told if you hope to succeed
    The truth will last as long as it has to
    The truth wants to be told, what will you do
The truth lives in each and every one of us
The truth really lives, but who will you trust
    The truth is the foundation of all things positive
    The truth is the foundation but to whom will you give
The truth is seen when you forget what you saw
The truth is seen when you're not sure who you are
    The truth always seems to find the right way
    The truth always will, when you won't that day
The truth will stand when others are gone
The truth will stand when you're on your own
    The truth is the truth there's nothing else to say
    The truth is the truth because god made it that way

THE TRUTH

The truth needs to be in you, and everything you do.
The truth will never follow you, but has a desire to always too.

The truth is the last words to be said, although it sits on the tip of your tongue.
The truth will never lie to you they cannot exist as one.

The truth can be spoken through lips with highest esteem.
The truth spoken in anger, will surely shattes precious dreams.

The truth looking from the outside sees not crystal clear.
The truth lived from the inside; allows you to walk through the fear.

The truth will always know the truth about you, and everything you do.
The truth can only hope you'll allow it to be a part of you.

The truth when you know it clears the clouds so you can see.
The truth when you hold it will always set you free.

THE WAY LOVE GOES

Looking for love and you won't give up, so love kisses your face a wet one but you always take it too far...past the point of no return, life lessons never learned.

Love flickers few warning signs but it was this November and she was getting colder and colder.
It was past the point of frost bite but that was alright you were determined to hold her tight.

Love never gives up what you want without a fight, love laughs in your face when in the dark where you can't see her, the same places where you keep trying to meet her.

Still wanting to hold her, love allowed you to have what you want but not what it needed, the cost was to be paid much later.
After you had love and held love, you tried to keep love to yourself, love slipped right away.

You now shed a few tears I suppose...not you but everyone else knows That's the way love sometimes goes.

THEM FRIENDS

Them friends
        Yours and mine
                Somebody she knows
                        Knows a friend of mine
                                His cousin, her brother
                                        They knew all of them too
                                                Now that we know each other
                                                What will we do

Some of us are old, some are brand new
        One is close to 100, yet another is less than 2
                A few are real tall, but more are like you and me
                        Now when we all come together it's like we're family
                                They say they know us, but how much of that is true
                                        I've never seen them, so they must only know you

THOUGHT I TOLD YOU

Didn't I tell u just don't go
    And didn't I tell u she's just a show
Didn't I tell u u can't win
    And didn't I tell u she aint your friend
Didn't I tell u to leave her alone
    And didn't I tell u don't take her home
Didn't I tell u not to do that
    And didn't I tell u she aint that phat
Didn't I tell u 2 keep your eyes open
    And didn't I tell u he aint joking
Didn't I tell u just stay down
    And didn't I tell u I heard a click sound
Didn't I tell u she aint worth that
    And didn't I tell u 2 drop that little bat
Didn't I tell u she was no good
    And didn't I tell u but u did what u could
Didn't I tell u bad things will soon end
    And didn't I tell u when he brought another friend
Didn't I tell u to take him to the ground
    And didn't I tell u I just heard a pop-pop sound
Didn't I tell u it was time so let's go
    I thought I told u so u can't say u didn't know

'TIL FOREVER YOURS

Time and time again who needs who,
Why do we do what we do
But still I wonder.
What must it be that drives me on and on,
Yet is this the right direction to go?
The destiny is still unknown.
Will it ever end?
Never is the answer I hear ringing in my ear.
Even though I wonder I still progress.
I grow in strength and will, yet still
I wonder not lost, but still.
One, two, give me three steps at a time.
Where shall I go,
Am I to really know when the way is dark yet
I am not blind.
Do what I must but still I wonder.
I did not; never dare not stop
But press on for now....'til forever yours!

TIME AND TIME AGAIN

Who needs who, why do we do what we do. But
Still I wonder

What must it be that drives men on yet is it in
The right direction?

The destiny is still unknown, will it ever end?
Never is the answer I hear ringing in my ear.

Even though I wonder, I still progress. I grow in
Strength and will.

Yet still I wonder lost, no but still unsure,
One, two, maybe three steps at a time.

Where shall I go, am I to really know, when the
Way is dark, yet I am not blind.

Do what I must, but still I wonder. I do not, no
Dare not stop, but press on for forever.

TIME UP

Running out of time the clock's ticking fast got to make a big move need to make more cash.

Done heard everything there is to know, talking's all over got to make that doe.

Pressed up against the wall just about to holla, could do almost anything for that mighty dollar.

Knowing I knew better and did it anyway, aint living for tomorrow got to make it today.

The lord's help is the only way I make it, only blind faith left just got to take it.

So when it's all said and I'm still standing, led not unto your own understanding.

But let it be known how this all came about, GOD's mighty hand came down and helped

This poor brother out, and if you don't know by now you need to think again

Because no one could help you more when GOD is your friend.

TO BE OR NOT TO BE

Looking at these people like they're looking at me
Reaching for the things they're holding for free.
Working real hard like it's nothing at all
Getting up and running after taking a fall
Holding all the good cards just about to win
Shudder to think you got nine but it takes ten
Reaching out for things only using one hand
Leaning over the edge, still moving from where we stand
Opening your mouth to talk, but nothing comes out
Listening for untold secrets a few know about
Standing on the top looking from near to far
They say they understand, but know not who you are
Keeping up with time as it ticks from within
The last breath you took was the beginning not the end
Crystal sky blue opens up to the stars
Like the midnight of darkness creeps behind locked bars
When there's nothing left to ponder, your will is all but done
It's to whom you give the glory that tells who truly won

(TOLD IT)
(TOLD IT)
(TOLD IT)
(TOLD IT)
(TOLD IT)
(TOLD IT)
ITS DONE

TOLD YOU SO

They didn't want to admit that I was right but they did.
Thought what I said was wrong, so they hide
But hiding won't change the fact of what was done.

Told about some things that ran around in my head
But everything I said just had to be said.
Nothing was left out every word was spoken
Better listen up close don't think I'm joking

Just like I told you before I'll tell you again
Thinking he's your buddy but he ain't no friend
Smiling and grinning up to no good talking "bout
I'm your boy, we from the hood.

Now everybody looking, looking cause it might be too late
Step back bro that's po-po putting up the yellow tape.
Everyone knew it, I mean everyone but you, now you stuck
In a situation so what you gonna do.

No time to cry now, better get while the gettin' is good
Get everything you can and everything you should.
He was dippin' and dodging right in your face, better
Check him now before you catch a case

Those hints to the wise, I guess just wasn't sufficient.
Like he was the one to start it, but who gonna finish it.
Never thought it could be like that, never thought that he would.
Now we know the truth and all the truth ain't good.

But hey, who am i to say what you should or shouldn't do.
It could have been me too, looking like boo-boo.
Just like they didn't tell you when the school bell was about to ring,
      Here comes po-po cause the fat lady is about to sing.

TRUE LOVE

Love never dies, so only fools can live forever
Love will be a tool for fools, until it can hurt no more
Love feeds my soul so that I can grow wiser
Love can't hurt with hate like we do, yet we still feel the pain
The best of love asks to be tested and some will pass with flying colors
Love needs me like we need us, but only love knows why
I need love to just let me be me
Love is why men won't cry and a woman's tears will fill the ocean
Love never asks how I do it; it just knows that I did
Love won't care if it costs a lot; it just needs you to pay the cost
Love keeps water in my eyes, and then I always dry up my heart
Love sees us wanting her embrace, and then allows us to break from her
chains
Some will say that love never plays fair, that's because love never plays by
any rules

WHAT

Just do it
>**Did**

Been there
>**Came right back**

Come and get it
>**Yesterday**

Like bread and butter
>**Naw; grits and ham**

Yellow gold
>**Platinum ice**

Do it right now
>**Think more than twice**

Some time winner
>**Never a loser**

Gone 4 a minute
>**Here 2 stay**

Wasted memories
>**Put away**

Overnight success
>**Still to be**

Slipped real low
>**Now standing on top**

Luke warm waters
>**Steam red hot**

WHAT I KNOW

I know sometimes I can see without seeing, but still find it hard to know where I'm going.

I know on cloudy days when the wind is lightly blowing I can figure out who the   clouds look like, but not know you when you walk by.

I know what you and everyone else needs to do, but can't fix myself, and I'm good at it.

I know you don't understand me when I talk, but I can hear you loud and clear, so I just keep on talking.

I know your today is good and it lasted forever, but my yesterday is gone, my tomorrow hasn't got here, and it defiantly has to be better

I know if you should fall down each day you'll get back up, but I know I'll need some help after the third time.

I know we both have been through some ups and downs, but together you, me, and the master, we will conquer it all.

I know these things I'm telling you are so diverse and deep, but I don't want to seem   like I'm talking over your head.

I know you would do the same things I do if you could, but I think that you think I don't want you to be successful.

I know why your vision seems distant and blurry, but I'm still afraid to open both   eyes.

I know it doesn't take much for you, but I think I won't stop until I'm completely satisfied.

I know you still think I'm a good man, but I will be much greater if you could   understand that it's more than just me.

I know you wished upon a star and waited for it to happen, but now you know you've got to go get it yourself.

I know at first you thought I didn't know, but now you know better and we both know a lot more than we knew before.

BECAUSE NOW YOU KNOW!

WHAT I WILL BE

I thought I knew why I cried at night, holding my pillow tight but I didn't.

I knew I knew something wasn't right, yet I gave up without a fight, so here I sit.

Knowing that as it may be is not enough to end what I can't see so I wonder.

Now thinking around in circles will not get you to where you really want to be.

You can see the long distance you have traveled without truly going anywhere yet still feel you are complete. How much further can you go?

Is what you want, worth all of that or is it all still just a dream, not as real as it may seem. Then dream on dreamer. As for me I'm moving on to another level, one that was thought unreachable before.

I know everything is not for everybody and everybody can't do everything, but somebody

will when somebody else won't, and anybody can but most everybody don't.

So as you sit, I'm going to stand and if I fall I know where I'll land. So when I get up I'll be much taller. I won't see you cause you'll look smaller.

I will soar with the Eagles where I'm supposed to be and when you look up you'll see me. Don't be mad because I did what I do you had the same chance like me, didn't you.

WHAT'S IT ABOUT

Often talked about, but understood by a few.
Rose in the temple not sitting in the pew.

Thought very deeply about the things I never told.
Still doing time from the truth not made to unfold.

Started real late didn't get an early start.
Had many little pieces, but missed a big part.

Staring at the hour glass trying to see time pause.
Trying to run through life didn't hear god's call

Blessed with many material things, about to get a lot more.
The devil tried to do it, but the price Jesus paid for.

Down on my knees I just began to pray
And ask for forgiveness of all my sins today

Didn't know if god heard me, didn't know if I really understood,
Can't stop to think about it, just did the best I could.

Now standing in victory, but not standing all alone,
Pressed toward the high mark, didn't make it on my own.

So if you start to wonder and maybe you should.
Does god really love me like he said he would?

You need only breathe the air that you do
And then you too my brother will know like I do!!

WHAT'S LOVE LIKE

Love is like being blind folded in a pitch black dark room
Even when she lets you see, what really can you see.
NOTHING FROM NOTHING

Love is like you first hot ball candy
It gets worse before it gets better
BURN BABY BURN

Love is like wearing a shoe a half size too small
Her beauty overrides the pain that is sure to come
NO PAIN NO GAIN

Love is like staring at the sun with one eye closed
She may kiss the other one open but the both will see the same nothing
WHAT YOU SEE IS WHAT YOU GET

Love is like a blinking red light;
She makes you stop to make sure when you think you can make it
BLINDED BY HER LIGHT

Love is like the window shopping you do in your head
She's wishing you could afford her too
IT WAS JUST YOUR IMAGINATION

Love is like eating all the chocolate you shouldn't have
She's going to cost you more than what you think
YOU COULD PAY NOW BUT YOU WILL PAY LATER

Love is like a real nice dream
She lasted a lot longer than you thought she would
IF YOU THINK YOU'RE LONELY NOW

Love is like an overnight guest that just stayed too long
She knows why she came, didn't you
YOU CAN GET WITH THIS OR YOU CAN GET WITH THAT

Love is like your favorite rerun shows
She loves to be seen again and again
Even though we both know how it's going to end
IF LOVING YOU IS WRONG I DON'T WANT TO BE RIGHT

Love is like that so I just think its best that I just let love be

WHICH WAY TO GO

Enchanted by the rhythm, trapped by its smile.
Captured by its beauty wanting to stay a while.

In and out of memories, while still standing by the door
Asking for fulfillness yet still wanting more.

Looking for some answers, though a few you already knew.
If you asked these questions then what will you do?

Tempted to dig a little deeper yet already knowing the truth.
While not wanting to grow older still holding on to your youth.

Scared to move forward as if you missed the dance.
Not really wanting to know, if this is your last chance.

Listen for the music when played nice and slow.
Now look toward the heavens, he'll tell you then you'll know.

WHO IS HE

Who is he is sometimes asked
To explain all he's done is no easy task

He has turned the lights on when the way was dark
He has washed me clean and removed any mark

When the mountain was steep and hard to climb
He pulled me up more than one more time

When everyone turned and walked away
He stayed right there day after day

You may not know this person of whom I speak
He's made you strong when you were weak

If you ask it shall be done
You need to know him the Father's son

WINNING

In spite of what it seems to be, things aren't what they use to be, and will be much better.

As the years do move by me, stacked up high where you can't see, the life you live does really matter.

For when you pause while thinking a bit, good things will happen as you commit to win the game no matter.

All is gained through conquered pain that changes the chosen battle.

Who are we, that's you and me and the people who chose to become better.

Life lessons learned makes funny turns that open doors for those who chose to enter.

It's not often known how much we've grown until pushed to a higher level.

Looking from the bottom the top seems such a lonely trail but walking the walk while talking the talk, who was I to tell.

Stay focused on the task at hand. Press into that Promised Land. Then lend a hand to a fellow man who listened to your story.

Inspired by more than what you knew, still many eyes are watching you as you press through to live for tomorrow.

Win from within.

ABOUT THE AUTHOR

Mr. Kirk Hollowell is a dedicated leader and family man who served in the US army in Wiesbaden Germany. Kirk works as a Manager with 3DI/LLC a local company in Newport News Va. and lives in Hampton Va. He is the father of an adult daughter and son and the grandfather of two awesome grandchildren.

www.ingramcontent.com/pod-product-compliance
Lightning Source LLC
Chambersburg PA
CBHW031520040426
42445CB00009B/315